ONE-POT

ONE-POT

Simple recipes for hearty, slow-cooked meals

CONTENTS

RECIPES 6

Guide to symbols

The recipes in this book are accompanied by symbols that alert you to important information.

 Tells you how many people the recipe serves, or how much is produced.

 Indicates how much time you will need to prepare and cook a dish. Next to this symbol you will also find out if additional time is required for such things as marinating, standing, proving, or cooling. You need to read the recipe to find out exactly how much extra time is needed.

 Alerts you to what has to be done before you can begin to cook the recipe, or to parts of the recipe that take a long time to complete.

 Denotes that special equipment is required. Where possible, alternatives are given.

❄ Accompanies freezing information.

Red lentil and tomato soup

With a hint of chilli, this is a thick, warming soup.

INGREDIENTS

2 tbsp olive oil
2 onions, finely chopped
4 garlic cloves, grated or finely chopped
pinch of chilli flakes
4 carrots, finely chopped
salt and freshly ground black pepper
450g (1lb) red lentils
3 x 400g cans chopped tomatoes
1.4 litres (2½ pints) hot vegetable stock

METHOD

1 Heat the oil in a large pan, add the onions, and cook over a low heat for 6–8 minutes, or until soft and translucent. Stir through the garlic, chilli flakes, and carrots, season with salt and pepper, and cook for 2 minutes.

2 Add the lentils, stir, then add the tomatoes and stock. Bring to the boil, then simmer on a very low heat for 35–40 minutes, or until the lentils are soft. Transfer to a blender or food processor and whiz until blended and smooth. Taste, and season with salt and pepper if needed.

3 To serve, transfer to a pan and heat until piping hot.

serves 8

prep 15 mins,
• cook 50 mins

blender or
food processor

freeze for up to 3 months;
defrost in the refrigerator
overnight, then reheat

Leek and potato soup

Potatoes give this homely soup body, while leeks lend a silky texture.

INGREDIENTS

2 tbsp olive oil

2 onions, finely chopped

salt and freshly ground black pepper

3 garlic cloves, grated or finely chopped

6 sage leaves, finely chopped

900g (2lb) leeks, cleaned and
  finely sliced

1.4 litres (2½ pints) hot vegetable stock

900g (2lb) potatoes, peeled and
  roughly chopped

150ml (5fl oz) double cream, to serve

METHOD

1 Heat the oil in a large pan, add the onions, and cook over a low heat for 6–8 minutes, or until soft and translucent. Season with salt and pepper, then stir in the garlic and sage. Add the leeks and stir well, then cook over a low heat for 10 minutes, or until the leeks are starting to soften.

2 Pour in the stock, bring to the boil, then add the potatoes and simmer for 20 minutes, or until soft. Transfer to a blender or food processor and whiz until blended and smooth. Taste, and season with salt and pepper if needed.

3 To serve, transfer to a pan, stir in the cream, and heat until piping hot.

serves 8

prep 15 mins
• cook 40 mins

blender or
food processor

freeze for up to 3 months;
defrost in the refrigerator
overnight, then reheat

Quick fish stew

This stew can be made even more quickly if you use cooked prawns instead of fresh ones.

INGREDIENTS

1 tbsp olive oil

1 onion, finely chopped

3 garlic cloves, grated or finely chopped

5 celery sticks, chopped

2 carrots, chopped

salt

sprig of thyme, leaves only

1 tsp tomato purée

1 glass of dry white wine

4 tomatoes, skinned

900ml (1½ pints) light fish stock

2 haddock fillets, about 675g (1½lb) total weight, cut into chunky pieces

200g (7 oz) raw prawns, peeled and deveined

handful of flat-leaf parsley, finely chopped

METHOD

1 Heat the oil in a pan over a low heat, and add the onion, garlic, celery, and carrots, along with a pinch of salt and the thyme. Sweat gently for about 10 minutes.

2 Now stir in the tomato purée, increase the heat to high, and add the wine. Let it simmer for a couple of minutes, then add the tomatoes (squashing them with a fork) and a little of the stock, and simmer a little more. Pour in almost all of the remaining stock, and bring to the boil. Reduce the heat slightly, and simmer for 10 minutes. At this point, you can blend the sauce with a hand-held blender until smooth, if you like. Top up with the remaining stock if needed.

3 Add the fish and prawns, cover the pan, and cook for 5–10 minutes until the fish is cooked through. Serve hot with fresh, crusty bread.

serves 4

prep 10 mins
• cook 30 mins

blender

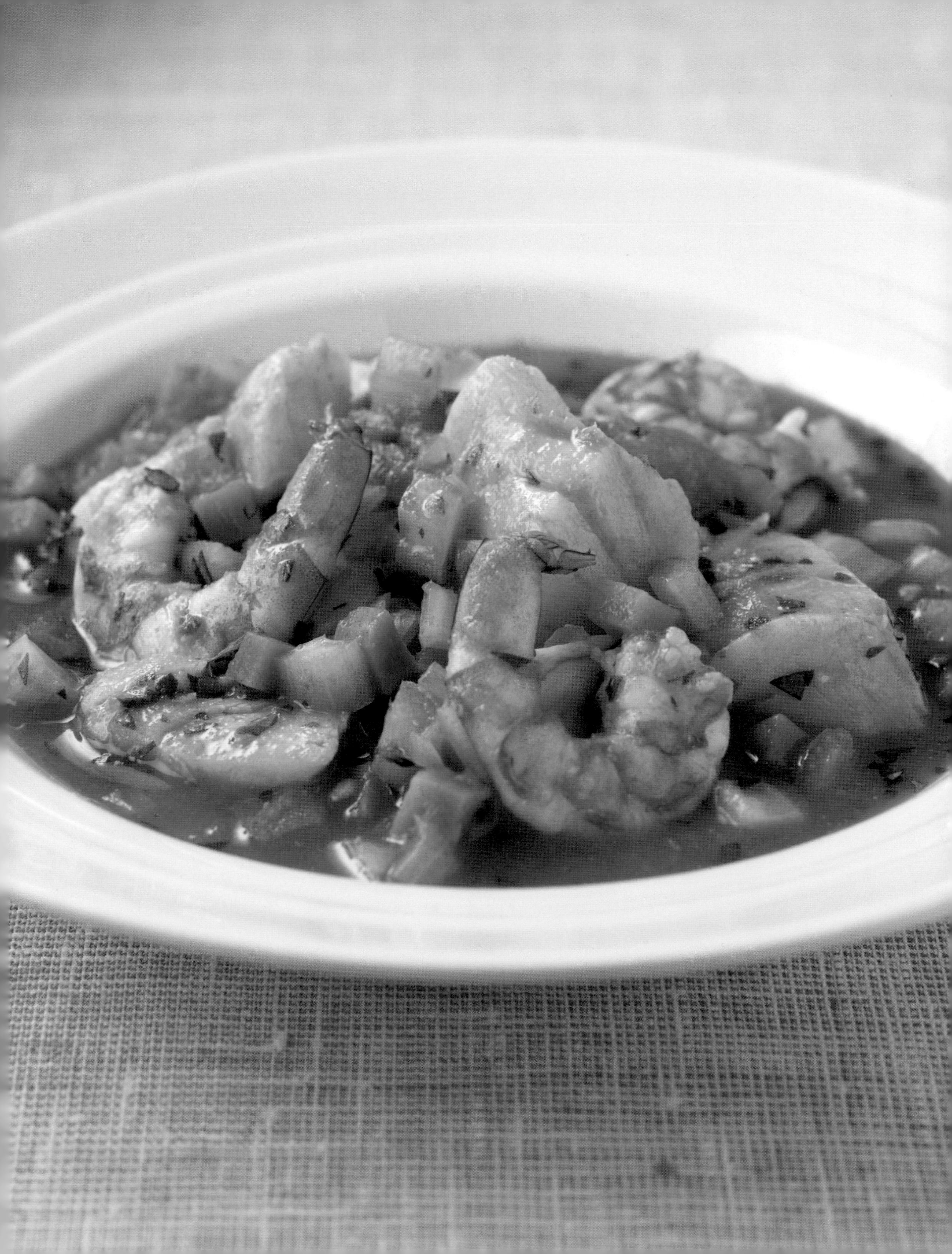

Prawn makhani

This creamy, spicy recipe is based on a classic curry from North India.

INGREDIENTS

700g (1lb 9 oz) (shelled weight) uncooked prawns, peeled and deveined

salt and freshly ground black pepper

6 garlic cloves, grated or finely chopped

15cm (6in) piece of fresh root ginger, peeled and grated, or finely chopped

3 tbsp vegetable oil

200ml (7fl oz) thick natural yogurt

2–3 tsp chilli powder

2 cinnamon sticks, broken into pieces

4 red chillies, deseeded and finely chopped

6 cardamom pods, crushed

700g (1lb 9 oz) tomatoes

125g (4½ oz) cashew nuts, ground, plus a handful, roughly chopped, to garnish

2–3 tsp ground fenugreek

200ml (7fl oz) double cream

METHOD

1 Season the prawns with salt and pepper and toss with half the garlic, half the ginger, 1 teaspoon of the oil, the yogurt, and chilli powder. Heat a large deep-sided frying pan, then add the prawns with as much of the yogurt coating as you can, and cook over a high heat, tossing them all the time, for 5–8 minutes, or until no longer pink. Remove and set aside.

2 Heat the remaining oil in the pan, add the rest of the ginger and garlic, the cinnamon, chillies, and cardamom pods, and cook over a low heat, stirring occasionally, for 2 minutes. Add the tomatoes and cook for 10 minutes, or until they start to reduce. Cover with a little hot water and simmer for a further 10 minutes, or until puréed.

3 Push the tomato mixture through a sieve into a food processor and whiz until smooth. Return to the pan, then stir through the ground cashew nuts and fenugreek and simmer for 10 minutes, adding a little hot water if the sauce starts to look too thick. Add the prawns along with the cream, stir, taste, and season, if needed. Cook for 5 minutes, then garnish with the chopped cashew nuts and serve with rice.

serves 8

prep 20 mins
• cook 40 mins

food processor

Pan-fried clams with parsley and garlic

A simple, Mediterranean-style sauce is all it takes to make the most of fresh clams.

INGREDIENTS

1 tbsp olive oil
1 onion, finely chopped
salt
2 garlic cloves, grated or finely chopped
1–2 green peppers, deseeded and
   finely chopped
1 large glass of dry white wine

450g (1 lb) fresh clams, rinsed well
   (discard any that have cracked or
   broken shells)
handful of flat-leaf parsley, finely
   chopped
lemon wedges, to serve (optional)

METHOD

1 Heat the oil in a large frying pan over a medium heat. Add the onion and a pinch of salt, and sweat for about 5 minutes until soft and translucent. Add the garlic and peppers, and gently sweat until the peppers begin to soften. Increase the heat to high, and add the wine. Cook for a couple of minutes until the wine begins to evaporate.

2 Add the clams, shaking the pan occasionally, and cook for 5–6 minutes until the clams open (discard any that do not). Add the parsley, and stir to combine. Serve piping hot with fresh crusty bread to mop up the juices and some lemon wedges for squeezing over (if using).

 serves 4

prep 10 mins
• cook 20 mins

before cooking, tap the
clams and discard any
that do not close

Smoked fish and anchovy gratin

A creamy and flavourful fish dish with a crisp, golden topping.

INGREDIENTS

125g (4½ oz) smoked
  mackerel
125g (4½ oz) smoked salmon
8–12 whole anchovies in
  oil, drained
4 waxy potatoes, peeled,
  boiled, and sliced
knob of butter, melted

For the sauce

knob of butter
1 onion, finely chopped
1 garlic clove, grated or finely chopped
1 tbsp plain flour
300ml (10fl oz) milk
salt and freshly ground black pepper
handful of curly-leaf parsley, finely chopped

METHOD

1 Preheat the oven to 200°C (400°F/Gas 6). To make the sauce, melt the butter in a pan over a low heat. Add the onion, and sweat gently for about 5 minutes until soft and translucent, then add the garlic and cook for a few seconds more. Remove from the heat, and stir through the flour using a wooden spoon, then add a little milk and beat until smooth.

2 Return the pan to the heat, and slowly add the rest of the milk, stirring until the sauce has thickened. Season well with salt and pepper, and stir through the parsley.

3 Layer the smoked fish and anchovies in an ovenproof dish, then spoon over the sauce and gently combine. Top with a layer of potatoes, brush with melted butter, and bake in the oven for 15–20 minutes until golden, crispy, and heated through. Serve with a crisp green salad.

serves 4

prep 10 mins
• cook 30 mins

Baked bream

This classic Iberian dish, *Besugo al Horno*, combines fish and potatoes.

INGREDIENTS

2 sea bream, about 600g (1lb 5oz) each
1 tbsp tapenade
2 lemon slices, thickly cut
juice of 1 lemon
3 tbsp olive oil
700g (1lb 9oz) potatoes, very
   thinly sliced
1 onion, thinly sliced

2 peppers, deseeded and sliced into
   thin rings
4 garlic cloves, chopped
2 tbsp chopped flat-leaf parsley
1 tsp hot paprika (pimentón picante)
120ml (4fl oz) dry white wine
salt and freshly ground black pepper

METHOD

1 Make 2 diagonal cuts on each side of the thickest part of both fish. Place in a non-metallic dish and spread the tapenade over the inside and outside of each fish. Tuck a lemon slice into the gills of each fish, drizzle with the lemon juice, and place in the refrigerator to marinate for 1 hour.

2 Preheat the oven to 190°C (375°F/Gas 5). Grease an ovenproof dish with 1 tablespoon of the olive oil. Layer half the potatoes in the dish, then the onions and peppers on top. Scatter with the garlic and parsley and sprinkle with the paprika, then layer the remaining potatoes on top. Drizzle over the remaining olive oil, and sprinkle with 2–3 tablespoons of water. Cover with foil and bake for 40 minutes, or until the potatoes are cooked and golden.

3 Increase the temperature to 220°C (425°F/Gas 7). Place the fish on top of the potatoes, pour over the wine, season with salt and pepper, and return to the oven, uncovered, for 20 minutes, or until the fish is cooked. Serve immediately.

serves 4

**prep 10 mins plus
marinating • cook 1 hr**

Smoked haddock with spinach and pancetta

This deliciously satisfying dish is great for a quick supper.

INGREDIENTS

15g (½ oz) butter, plus extra for greasing

1 tbsp olive oil

1 onion, finely chopped

100g (3½ oz) pancetta or bacon, chopped

450g (1lb) spinach

100g (3½ oz) crème fraîche

salt and freshly ground black pepper

75g (2½ oz) Parmesan cheese, grated

800g (1¾ lb) smoked fillets of haddock or cod, skinned

juice of ½ lemon

30g (1 oz) fresh breadcrumbs

METHOD

1 Preheat the oven to 190°C (375°F/Gas 5) and grease an ovenproof serving dish with butter. Melt the oil and butter together in a frying pan and fry the onion and pancetta or bacon for 5 minutes.

2 Add the spinach and stir until wilted, then stir in the crème fraîche, seasoning, and three-quarters of the Parmesan. Simmer until slightly thickened.

3 Spoon the spinach mixture into the ovenproof dish and place the fish on top. Sprinkle with the lemon juice. Scatter with breadcrumbs and the remaining Parmesan, and bake for 15–20 minutes, or until the fish is cooked through and flakes easily.

serves 6

prep 10 mins
• cook 15–20 mins

Sweet and sour prawns

Prawns stir-fried in a fragrant sauce flavoured
with chilli, garlic, and ginger.

INGREDIENTS

3 tbsp rice wine vinegar

2 tbsp clear honey

1 tbsp caster sugar

2 tbsp light soy sauce

2 tbsp tomato ketchup

2 tbsp vegetable oil

3 shallots, peeled and sliced

2cm (¾in) piece of fresh root ginger,
   peeled and grated

1 red chilli, deseeded and finely
   chopped

1 garlic clove, crushed

1 small carrot, cut into matchsticks

1 celery stick, cut into matchsticks

1 green pepper, deseeded and cut into
   strips

500g (1lb 2oz) raw tiger prawns, peeled
   and deveined

2 spring onions, sliced lengthways, to
   garnish

METHOD

1 Heat the first 5 ingredients together in a small saucepan, until the honey and
   sugar melt. Remove from the heat and set aside.

2 Heat the oil in a wok, add the shallots, ginger, chilli, garlic, carrot, celery, and
   green pepper and stir-fry for 4 minutes.

3 Add the prawns and stir-fry for a further 2 minutes or until the prawns turn pink.
   Pour in the vinegar-and-sugar mixture and stir-fry for 1 minute, or until the prawns
   and vegetables are coated and everything is heated through.

4 To serve, transfer to a platter and garnish with spring onions. Serve with boiled rice.

serves 4

prep 20 mins
• cook 10 mins

wok

Courgette, herb, and lemon tagine

A tasty vegetarian version of the famous Moroccan speciality.

INGREDIENTS

2 tbsp olive oil

2 red onions, finely chopped

salt and freshly ground black pepper

4 garlic cloves, grated or finely chopped

pinch of fennel seeds

pinch of ground cinnamon

2–3 tsp harissa (depending on taste), plus extra, to serve

4 preserved lemons, halved, pith removed, and halved again

2 x 400g cans whole tomatoes, chopped

1 head of broccoli, broken into florets

6 courgettes, sliced

juice of 1 lemon

handful of dill, finely chopped

400g (14 oz) couscous

handful of flat-leaf parsley, finely chopped

lemon wedges, to serve

METHOD

1 Heat half the oil in a large heavy-based pan, add the onions, and cook over a low heat for 8 minutes, or until soft and translucent. Season well with salt and pepper. Stir through the garlic, fennel seeds, cinnamon, harissa, and preserved lemons.

2 Add the tomatoes and stir well, crushing them with the back of a wooden spoon. Bring to the boil, then reduce to a simmer and cook over a low heat for 30–40 minutes. If the sauce starts to dry out, top up with a little hot water.

3 Cook the broccoli in a pan of boiling salted water for 3–5 minutes or until tender, then drain and refresh in cold water. Drain again and put to one side. Heat the remaining oil in another frying pan, add the courgettes, and season with salt and pepper. Cook over a low heat, stirring frequently, for 5 minutes, or until they start to colour a little. Add the lemon juice and stir the dill through.

4 Meanwhile, put the couscous in a large bowl and pour over just enough boiling water to cover it. Leave for 10 minutes, then fluff up with a fork and season well with salt and pepper. Add the broccoli and courgettes to the sauce and stir through the parsley. Serve with the couscous, lemon wedges, and a spoonful of harissa.

serves 8

prep 25 mins • cook 1 hr

Vegetarian leek and mushroom lasagne

Grated mushrooms add a meaty texture and chillies a pleasant heat to this dish.

INGREDIENTS

6 tbsp olive oil

4 large leeks, cut into 5mm (¼in) slices

550g (1¼lb) chestnut mushrooms, sliced

250g (9 oz) chestnut mushrooms, grated

2–3 red chillies, deseeded and finely chopped

6 garlic cloves, chopped

150ml (5fl oz) dry white wine

small handful of thyme leaves

2 tbsp plain flour

900ml (1½ pints) milk

350g (12 oz) Cheddar cheese, grated

6 tomatoes, roughly chopped, plus 1 extra, sliced

salt and freshly ground black pepper

450g (1lb) lasagne sheets

METHOD

1 Pre-heat the oven to 180°C (350°F/Gas 4). Heat the oil in a large heavy-based pan, add the leeks, and cook over a low heat, stirring frequently, for 5 minutes, or until starting to soften. Stir in the mushrooms and cook, stirring frequently, for 5 minutes, or until they release their juices. Add the chillies and garlic, and cook for 1 minute. Pour in the wine, raise the heat, and boil for 3 minutes while the alcohol evaporates.

2 Stir in the thyme, then add the flour and mix well. Add a little of the milk, mix well, then add the rest of the milk and cook for 5 minutes, stirring frequently. Add almost all the cheese (reserve some for the topping), remove from the heat, and combine well. Add the chopped tomatoes and season well with salt and pepper.

3 Put a 1cm (½in) layer of the mixture in the bottom of a large ovenproof dish, then cover evenly with a layer of the lasagne sheets. Pour in another layer of sauce and cover with lasagne. Repeat the process until all the sauce is used up – you need to finish with a layer of sauce. Top with the remaining cheese and the sliced tomato.

4 Place the dish in the oven for 30 minutes, or until browning on top and piping hot.

 serves 8

 prep 25 mins • cook 20 mins

 freeze, uncooked in its dish, for up to 3 months; cook straight from frozen for 30–40 mins to serve

Chicken casserole with herb dumplings

Serve this hearty winter dish with freshly steamed greens.

INGREDIENTS

1 tbsp plain flour
salt and freshly ground black pepper
8 chicken thighs and drumsticks
2 tbsp olive oil
2 carrots, sliced
2 leeks, sliced
2 celery sticks, sliced
½ swede, diced
500ml (16fl oz) chicken stock
2 tbsp Worcestershire sauce

For the dumplings

125g (4½ oz) self-raising flour
60g (2 oz) light suet, shredded
1 tbsp flat-leaf parsley, chopped
1 tsp dried mixed herbs
salt and freshly ground black pepper

METHOD

1 Season the flour with salt and pepper. Toss the chicken pieces in the flour to coat. Heat half the oil in the casserole and fry the chicken, turning often, for 6 minutes, or until brown all over. Remove and keep warm. Pour the fat from the casserole.

2 Add the remaining oil, carrots, leeks, celery, and swede to the casserole, and stir over the heat for 3–4 minutes to colour lightly. Return the chicken to the casserole, and add the stock and Worcestershire sauce. Bring to the boil, then reduce the heat, cover, and simmer for 20 minutes.

3 Meanwhile, to make the dumplings, place the flour in a bowl and stir in the suet, parsley, and dried herbs, and season with salt and pepper. Stir in 5–6 tablespoons of cold water, or just enough to make a soft, not sticky, dough. With lightly floured hands, divide into 12 balls.

4 Remove the casserole lid and arrange the dumplings over the top. Cover and simmer for a further 20 minutes, or until the dumplings are risen and fluffy. Serve in the casserole.

serves 4

prep 15 mins
• cook 50 mins

large flameproof casserole

freeze, without dumplings, for up to 3 months

Chicken cacciatore

This Italian dish translates as "hunter-style chicken", and is traditionally served with polenta.

INGREDIENTS

4 chicken legs, about 1.5kg (3lb 3oz) total weight
salt and freshly ground black pepper
2 tbsp olive oil
2 garlic cloves, sliced
1 medium onion, chopped
200ml (7fl oz) dry white wine
1 celery stick, chopped

200g (7 oz) button mushrooms, sliced
400g can chopped tomatoes
150ml (5fl oz) chicken stock
1 tbsp tomato purée
2 tsp chopped rosemary
2 tsp chopped sage
8 pitted black olives, halved

METHOD

1 Trim any excess fat from the chicken and season with salt and pepper. Heat half the oil in a large, heavy frying pan and fry the chicken in batches, until brown on all sides. Remove and keep hot. Pour the excess fat out of the pan.

2 Heat the remaining oil and add the garlic and onion. Fry gently for 3–4 minutes, to soften but not brown. Add the wine and boil for 1 minute. Stir in the celery, mushrooms, tomatoes, stock, tomato purée, rosemary, and sage.

3 Return the chicken to the pan, cover, and cook over a low heat for 30 minutes, or until the chicken is cooked through.

4 Remove the lid, add the olives, then cover and cook for a further 5–10 minutes. Serve hot.

serves 4

prep 20 mins
• cook 35–40 mins

flameproof casserole

Coq au vin

A French classic that is perfect for entertaining.

INGREDIENTS

2 tbsp plain flour
salt and freshly ground black pepper
1 large chicken, jointed
60g (2 oz) butter
125g (4½ oz) pancetta,
   cut into thick short strips
2 garlic cloves, crushed
1 carrot, cut into cubes
1 celery stick, roughly chopped
4 tbsp brandy or Cognac

750ml (1¼ pints) red wine,
   such as Burgundy or Beaujolais
1 bay leaf
4–5 sprigs of thyme
1 tbsp olive oil
450g (1lb) button onions
1 tsp brown sugar
1 tsp red wine vinegar
225g (8 oz) small mushrooms

METHOD

1 Season the flour with salt and pepper. Coat the chicken with 1 tablespoon of the seasoned flour. Melt half the butter in the casserole, add the chicken, and fry gently until golden brown on all sides.

2 Add the pancetta, garlic, carrot, and celery, and fry until softened. Add the remaining flour and cook for 1–2 minutes. Pour in the brandy and wine, stirring to remove any sediment from the bottom of the casserole. Add the bay leaf and thyme, bring to the boil, cover, and simmer for 1 hour.

3 Meanwhile, melt the rest of the butter with the olive oil in a frying pan. Add the onions and fry until just brown. Stir in the sugar, vinegar, and 1 tablespoon of water.

4 Add the onions and mushrooms to the chicken, and cook for another 30 minutes, or until the chicken is cooked through and the vegetables are tender.

5 Transfer the chicken and vegetables to a hot serving dish. Discard the bay leaf and thyme. Skim off any excess fat and boil the sauce for 3–5 minutes, or until reduced. Pour over the chicken and serve with mashed potatoes and green vegetables.

serves 4

prep 30 mins
• cook 1 hr
30 mins

large flameproof
casserole

freeze for up
to 3 months

Chicken jalfrezi

A spicy dish with chillies and mustard seeds, for those who like their curries hot.

INGREDIENTS

2 tbsp sunflower oil

2 tsp ground cumin

2 tsp yellow mustard seeds

1 tsp ground turmeric

2 tbsp masala curry paste

2.5cm (1in) piece fresh root ginger, peeled and finely chopped

3 garlic cloves, crushed

1 onion, sliced

1 red pepper, deseeded and sliced

½ green pepper, deseeded and sliced

2 green chillies, deseeded and finely chopped

675g (1½lb) skinless boneless chicken thighs or breasts, cut into 2.5cm (1in) pieces

225g can chopped tomatoes

3 tbsp chopped coriander

METHOD

1 Heat the oil in a large pan over a medium heat, add the cumin, mustard seeds, turmeric, and curry paste, and stir-fry for 1–2 minutes.

2 Add the ginger, garlic, and onion and fry, stirring frequently, until the onion starts to soften. Add the red and green peppers and the chillies and fry for 5 minutes.

3 Increase the heat to medium-high, add the chicken, and fry until starting to brown. Add the tomatoes and coriander, reduce the heat, and simmer for 10 minutes, or until the chicken is cooked through, stirring often. Serve hot with basmati rice and poppadums.

serves 4

prep 20 mins
• cook 25 mins

freeze for up to 3 months

Chicken chow mein

This popular Chinese dish is a colourful, tasty medley of noodles, chicken, mushrooms, and vegetables.

INGREDIENTS

4 tsp vegetable oil

4 spring onions, cut into 2.5cm (1in) lengths

2cm (¾in) piece of fresh root ginger, peeled and grated

140g (5 oz) shiitake mushrooms or oyster mushrooms, sliced

1 red pepper, deseeded and chopped

6 skinless boneless chicken thighs, cut into bite-sized pieces

115g (4 oz) green beans, cut into 2.5cm (1in) lengths

350g (12 oz) fresh fine egg noodles

4 tbsp light soy sauce, plus extra for sprinkling

1 tbsp rice wine or dry sherry

120ml (4fl oz) chicken stock

1 tsp cornflour

METHOD

1 Heat half the oil in a wok or large frying pan and stir-fry the spring onions, ginger, mushrooms, and red pepper over high heat for 5 minutes. Remove and set aside.

2 Add the remaining oil and stir-fry the chicken over a high heat for 3 minutes, in separate batches if necessary, then remove from the pan and set aside.

3 Add the green beans and stir-fry for 2 minutes. Add the noodles and return the chicken and vegetables to the pan.

4 Mix together the soy sauce, rice wine or dry sherry, stock, and cornflour until smooth and well blended, then pour into the pan. Toss everything together for 2 minutes, or until piping hot.

5 Serve immediately, with extra soy sauce to sprinkle over.

serves 4

prep 15 mins
• cook 15 mins

wok

Special fried rice

INGREDIENTS

900g (2lb) basmati rice
salt and freshly ground black pepper
5 tbsp sunflower oil
450g (1lb) (shelled weight) uncooked
  shrimps or prawns, peeled,
  deveined, and chopped
4 large skinless chicken fillets, cut into
  2.5cm (1in) strips
425g (15 oz) pancetta, cubed
225g (8 oz) white mushrooms, diced

7.5cm (3in) piece of fresh root ginger,
  peeled and finely sliced
225g (8 oz) frozen peas, defrosted
4 eggs, lightly beaten
2 tbsp dark soy sauce
2 tbsp mirin
1 bunch of spring onions, finely sliced
small handful of flat-leaf parsley, finely
  chopped

METHOD

1 Rinse the rice well, then place in a large pan, cover with boiling water, and add a pinch
  of salt. Cover with a lid, bring to the boil, and cook for 15–20 minutes, or until done.
  Drain well and put to one side to cool completely.

2 Meanwhile, heat 1 tablespoon of the oil in a wok over a high heat, add the shrimps or
  prawns, season with salt and pepper, and cook for 10 minutes, or until pink. Remove
  with a slotted spoon and put to one side. Heat another tablespoon of the oil in the wok,
  add the chicken, season with salt and pepper, and stir-fry for 10 minutes, or until no
  longer pink. Remove with a slotted spoon and put to one side.

3 Heat another tablespoon of the oil in the wok, add the pancetta, and cook over a
  medium-high heat for 6–8 minutes, or until crispy and golden. Remove with a slotted
  spoon and put to one side. Wipe the wok out with kitchen paper, then heat another
  tablespoon of the oil in it. Add the mushrooms and ginger, and stir-fry for 5 minutes, or
  until the mushrooms start to soften. Add the peas for the last minute or two. Remove
  with a slotted spoon and put to one side.

4 Heat the remaining oil in the wok, then pour in the eggs and cook gently, stirring them
  around the pan, for 1 minute. Take care not to overcook them. Add the rice and stir well,
  then stir in the shrimps or prawns, the chicken, pancetta, mushrooms, and peas. Add
  the soy sauce and mirin and cook for 5 minutes, stirring all the time. Transfer to a large
  shallow serving dish, top with the spring onions and parsley, and serve.

serves 8

prep 15 mins,
plus cooling
• cook 40 mins

wok

Navarin of lamb

This classic French stew is traditionally made with young spring vegetables.

INGREDIENTS

15g (½ oz) butter

1 tbsp olive oil

900g (2lb) middle neck of lamb, cut into pieces

2 small onions, quartered

1 tbsp plain flour

400ml (14fl oz) lamb stock or beef stock

2 tbsp tomato purée

1 bouquet garni

salt and freshly ground black pepper

300g (10 oz) small new potatoes

300g (10 oz) small whole carrots

300g (10 oz) baby turnips

175g (6 oz) French beans

METHOD

1 Melt the butter with the oil in a large flameproof casserole, add the lamb, and fry until brown on all sides. Add the onions and fry gently for 5 minutes, stirring frequently.

2 Sprinkle the flour over the meat and stir well for 2 minutes, or until the pieces are evenly coated. Stir in the stock, then add the tomato purée and bouquet garni, and season to taste with salt and pepper. Bring to the boil, then cover and simmer for 45 minutes.

3 Add the potatoes, carrots, and turnips. Cover and cook for a further 15 minutes, then stir in the beans, cover, and cook for a further 10–15 minutes, or until all the vegetables are tender.

serves 4

prep 30 mins • cook 1 hr 30 mins

large flameproof casserole

freeze for up to 3 months

Irish stew

Made with lamb and potatoes, this dish is slow-cooked for maximum flavour and tenderness.

INGREDIENTS

8 best-end neck of lamb chops,
  about 750g (1lb 10 oz) total weight
800g (1¾lb) onions, sliced
3 carrots, thickly sliced
800g (1¾lb) floury potatoes,
  peeled and thickly sliced
salt and freshly ground black pepper
large sprig of thyme
1 bay leaf
600ml (1 pint) lamb stock or beef stock

METHOD

1 Preheat the oven to 160°C (325°F/Gas 3).
2 Layer the lamb, onions, carrots, and one-third of the potato slices in a large, heavy casserole. Season with salt and pepper between the layers.
3 Tuck the thyme and bay leaf into the ingredients, then top with the remaining potato slices. Pour the stock over, cover, and place in the oven for 1 hour.
4 Remove the lid and return the casserole to the oven for a further 30–40 minutes, or until the top is browned. Serve hot, with a fresh green vegetable, such as spring greens, kale, or broccoli.

serves 4–6

prep 20 mins
• cook 1 hr 40 mins

Lamb tagine with couscous

The dried apricots, cumin, coriander, ginger, and thyme that flavour this dish are typical of Moroccan cuisine.

INGREDIENTS

1 onion, thinly sliced

1 tsp ground coriander

1 tsp ground cumin

1 tsp ground ginger

1 tsp dried thyme

2 tbsp sunflower oil or peanut oil

900g (2lb) boneless lamb, such as
   shoulder or chump steaks, cut into
   2.5cm (1in) cubes

2 tbsp plain flour

300ml (10fl oz) orange juice

600ml (1 pint) chicken stock

115g (4 oz) no-soak dried apricots

salt and freshly ground black pepper

mint leaves, to garnish

200g (7 oz) quick-cook couscous

salt

METHOD

1 Put the onion, coriander, cumin, ginger, thyme, and 1 tablespoon of the oil in a large, non-metallic bowl, then mix in the lamb. Cover and refrigerate for at least 3 hours or overnight to marinate.

2 When ready to cook, preheat the oven to 160°C (325°F/Gas 3). Put the flour in a small bowl and slowly stir in the orange juice until smooth, then set aside.

3 Heat the remaining oil in a large, flameproof casserole over a high heat. Add the lamb mixture and fry, stirring frequently, for 5 minutes, or until browned.

4 Stir the orange juice mixture into the casserole with the stock. Bring to the boil, stirring, then remove the casserole from the heat, cover, and place in the oven for 1 hour.

5 Remove the casserole from the oven. Stir in the apricots, cover and return to the oven. Cook for a further 20 minutes, or until the lamb is tender.

6 Meanwhile, put the couscous with a pinch of salt in a large heatproof bowl and pour over 2.5cm (1in) of boiling water. Cover with a folded tea towel and leave to stand for 10 minutes, or until the grains are tender. Fluff with a fork and keep warm. When the lamb is tender, taste and adjust the seasoning. Sprinkle with mint leaves and serve the lamb with the hot couscous.

 serves 4

 prep 10 mins, plus marinating • cook 1 hr 30

 marinate for at least 3 hrs

 large flameproof casserole

 freeze for up to 1 month

Slow-cooked Greek lamb

Roast lamb is popular at Easter in Greece.

INGREDIENTS

1.35kg (3lb) leg of lamb
2 tbsp olive oil
3 garlic cloves, crushed
1 tsp ground cinnamon
1 tsp dried thyme
1 tsp dried oregano or marjoram
juice of 1 lemon
1 tsp freshly ground black pepper
1 onion, sliced into rings
2 carrots, halved lengthways
2 tbsp chopped flat-leaf parsley

METHOD

1 Preheat the oven to 150°C (300°F/Gas 2). Place the lamb in a roasting tin. Mix the oil, garlic, cinnamon, and dried herbs, and brush over the lamb. Sprinkle with the lemon juice and season with pepper.

2 Half-fill the tin with water, and add the onion and carrots. Cook for 3 hours, basting every 30 minutes, and topping up the water if necessary.

3 Cover with foil and cook for another 1½–2 hours, or until the meat comes away from the bone.

4 Remove from the oven, and leave to rest for 20 minutes before serving. Arrange the lamb on a platter with parsley scattered over.

serves 4

prep 10 mins, plus resting
• cook 4½–5 hrs

Cassoulet

INGREDIENTS

350g (12 oz) dried haricot beans
1 tbsp olive oil
8 Toulouse sausages
250g (9 oz) piece of pancetta,
  cut into small pieces
2 onions, peeled and finely chopped
1 carrot, peeled and chopped
4 garlic cloves, crushed
4 duck legs

1 sprig of thyme, plus ½ tbsp
  chopped leaves
1 bay leaf
salt and freshly ground black pepper
2 tbsp tomato purée
400g can chopped tomatoes
200ml (7fl oz) white wine
½ day-old baguette
1 tbsp chopped flat-leaf parsley

METHOD

1 Place the beans in a pan, cover with plenty of cold water, bring to the boil, and boil for 10 minutes. Remove from the heat and soak for 2–3 hours, then drain.

2 Heat the olive oil in a frying pan and brown the sausages for 7–8 minutes, turning occasionally. Remove from the pan and set aside. Add the pancetta to the pan, and cook for 5 minutes. Remove and set aside with the sausages. Add the onions and carrot, and cook gently for 10 minutes, or until soft. Then add three-quarters of the garlic and cook for 1 minute.

3 Preheat the oven to 220°C (425°F/Gas 7). Prick the duck legs all over with a fork, place in a roasting tin, and roast for 30 minutes. Remove from the oven. Reserve the duck fat, and reduce the oven to 140°C (275°F/Gas 1).

4 In the casserole, layer the ingredients, beginning with half the beans, then onions, carrot, sausages, pancetta, and duck legs, followed by the remaining beans. Push the thyme sprig and bay leaf in among everything and season well with salt and pepper.

5 Mix together 900ml (1½ pints) hot water with the tomato purée, tomatoes, and wine, then pour into the casserole. Cover, and cook in the oven for 3 hours, adding a little extra water if required.

6 Cut the crusts off the baguette, then tear the bread into pieces and place in a food processor with the remaining garlic. Process into coarse crumbs. Heat 2 tablespoons of the duck fat in a frying pan and fry the crumbs over a medium heat for 7–8 minutes, or until crisp and golden. Drain on kitchen paper and stir in the parsley. Remove the cassoulet from the oven and stir. Sprinkle the breadcrumb topping over in a thick, even layer, and serve.

serves 4–6

prep 30 mins,
plus soaking
• cook 3 hrs
45 mins

allow 2–3 hrs
for soaking
the beans

3.5-litre (6-pint)
flameproof casserole
• food processor

Hungarian goulash

This warming winter stew makes a great main course if you are entertaining, as all the hard work can be done in advance.

INGREDIENTS

4 tbsp oil
900g (2lb) braising steak, cut into
  2.5cm (1in) cubes
2 large onions, thinly sliced
2 garlic cloves, crushed
2 red peppers, deseeded and chopped
1 tbsp paprika, plus extra to garnish

400g can chopped tomatoes
2 tbsp tomato purée
1 tbsp plain flour
300ml (10fl oz) beef stock
1 tsp chopped thyme
salt and freshly ground black pepper
150ml (5fl oz) soured cream

METHOD

1 Preheat the oven to 160°C (325°F/Gas 3).

2 Heat half the oil in a large frying pan and brown the meat in batches, transferring to a large casserole as they finish browning.

3 Add the remaining oil to the pan, lower the heat, and fry the onions, garlic, and peppers until soft. Stir in the paprika and cook for 1 minute, then add the tomatoes and tomato purée. Mix the flour with a little stock until smooth, then pour it into the pan with the rest of the stock. Bring to the boil, stirring often. Add the thyme, season to taste with salt and pepper, then pour the sauce into the casserole.

4 Cover tightly and place in the oven for 2 hours, or until the beef is very tender.

5 To serve, spoon the goulash into individual bowls and top each serving with a couple of spoonfuls of soured cream and sprinkle with a little paprika. Goulash is delicious served with buttered tagliatelle.

serves 4

prep 25 mins
• cook 2 hrs
30 mins

freeze, without the
soured cream, for
up to 3 months

Pork and bean stew

INGREDIENTS

500g (1lb 2oz) dried black-eyed beans
2 pig's trotters
250g (9 oz) smoked pork ribs
175g (6 oz) smoked streaky bacon,
   left in 1 piece
200g can chopped tomatoes
1 tbsp tomato purée
1 bay leaf
salt and freshly ground black pepper

oil, for frying
500g (1lb 2oz) lean pork fillet or steaks
1 small onion, finely chopped
2 garlic cloves, finely chopped
175g (6 oz) chorizo sausage, cut into
   small chunks
1 green chilli, deseeded (optional)
1 orange, cut into wedges, to garnish
3 spring onions, chopped, to garnish

METHOD

1 Rinse the beans, place in a bowl, and pour over cold water to cover. Leave overnight.

2 Drain the beans and place in a large saucepan. Cover with fresh water, bring to the boil, and boil for 10 minutes, skimming off any scum, then lower the heat, cover and simmer for 1 hour.

3 Meanwhile, place the pig's trotters, pork ribs, and streaky bacon in a saucepan with the canned tomatoes and their juice, the tomato purée, bay leaf, and salt and pepper to taste. Add enough cold water to cover, bring to the boil, skim off any scum, cover, reduce the heat and simmer for 50 minutes.

4 Drain the beans and reserve the cooking liquid, then return the beans to the pan. Add the meats with their cooking liquid. Add just enough of the reserved cooking liquid from the beans to cover. Continue to cook, covered, over a low heat, for another 20 minutes.

5 Heat 1 tablespoon of oil in a frying pan and brown the pork fillet. Add to the meat and bean mixture and continue to cook for a further 10 minutes, or until the meat is tender and the beans very soft. Wipe out the frying pan, add 1 tablespoon of oil and fry the onion and garlic over medium heat for 3–4 minutes, stirring frequently, until soft and translucent. Add the chorizo and chilli, if using, and fry for a further 2 minutes, stirring. Add 2–3 tablespoons of the cooked beans to the frying pan and mash well with the back of a spoon. Add the contents of the frying pan to the meat and beans, stir, and cook for a further 10 minutes.

6 To serve, remove the larger pieces of meat and cut into smaller pieces. Transfer them and the rest of the meat and bean mixture on to a serving dish and garnish with orange wedges and spring onions. Serve immediately.

 serves 6–8

 prep 1 hr 15 mins,
plus soaking
• cook 1 hr 35 mins

 the beans need
to be soaked
the day before

Chicken with broad beans

This easy recipe is also versatile: try it with good-quality sausages for a variation.

INGREDIENTS

8 chicken thighs
salt and freshly ground black pepper
2 tbsp olive oil
1 onion, finely chopped
2 celery sticks, finely chopped
2 garlic cloves, grated or finely chopped

a few sprigs of rosemary, leaves picked and finely chopped
1 large glass of dry white wine
200g (7 oz) frozen broad beans, or fresh if in season
500ml (16fl oz) hot chicken stock

METHOD

1 Preheat the oven to 200°C (400°F/Gas 6). Season the chicken pieces well with salt and black pepper. Heat 1 tablespoon of the oil in a large flameproof casserole over a medium-high heat. Add the chicken, skin-side down, and brown for 5–6 minutes on each side until golden all over. Remove from the pan, and set aside.

2 Reduce the heat to low, and add the remaining oil to the casserole. Add the onion and a pinch of salt, and sweat for 5 minutes until soft. Now add the celery, garlic, and rosemary, and sweat for a further 5 minutes. Increase the heat, pour in the wine, and let simmer for about 5 minutes.

3 Stir through the broad beans, and return the chicken to the pan, tucking the pieces in and around the beans. Pour the stock over, cover, and cook in the oven for 45 minutes to 1 hour. Check halfway through the cooking time, topping up with a little hot water if too dry. Serve with oven-roasted tomatoes and fresh crusty bread.

serves 4

**prep 10 mins
• cook 1 hr**

large flameproof casserole

Blanquette de veau

A simple, delicately flavoured stew.

INGREDIENTS

675g (1½lb) veal shoulder or leg, boned, trimmed, and diced

2 onions, roughly chopped

2 carrots, peeled and chopped

1 tbsp lemon juice

1 bouquet garni (6 parsley stalks, 1 bay leaf, 1 celery stalk, 5 black peppercorns, and 3 thyme sprigs, tied in muslin)

salt and freshly ground black pepper

85g (3 oz) butter

18 white pearl onions

225g (8 oz) brown cap mushrooms, quartered

2 tbsp plain white flour

1 egg yolk

2–3 tbsp single cream

flat-leaf parsley, chopped, to garnish

METHOD

1 Put the veal, onions, carrots, lemon juice, and bouquet garni in the casserole with enough water to cover. Season with salt and pepper. Simmer over a low heat for 1 hour, or until the meat is tender.

2 Meanwhile, melt 25g (scant 1 oz) of the butter in a frying pan over a medium heat. Add the onions and fry, stirring occasionally, until golden. Add another 25g (scant 1 oz) of butter and the mushrooms. Fry for 5 minutes, or until soft, stirring occasionally.

3 Strain off the cooking liquid from the veal, reserving 600ml (1 pint). Add the meat and vegetables to the mushrooms and onions, then set aside, and keep warm.

4 Melt the remaining butter in a large pan. Add the flour and stir constantly for 1 minute. Remove the pan from the heat and gradually stir in the reserved liquid. Return the pan to the heat and bring the sauce to the boil, stirring, until it thickens.

5 Adjust the seasoning to taste, remove the pan from the heat, and let it cool slightly. Beat the egg yolk and cream in a small bowl, then slowly stir it into the sauce. Add the meat and vegetables and reheat, without boiling, for 5 minutes. Season, garnish with parsley, and serve.

serves 4

prep 15 mins • cook 1 hr 30 mins

muslin • large flameproof casserole

Quick lamb curry

This is a great way to use up leftover lamb. The amount of curry powder can be adjusted to taste.

INGREDIENTS

1 onion, quartered

3 garlic cloves, sliced

2.5cm (1in) piece of fresh root ginger, peeled and chopped

2 green peppers, deseeded and quartered

1 green chilli, deseeded

2 tbsp oil

1 tbsp black mustard seeds

1–2 tbsp curry powder

400g can chopped tomatoes

100g (3½ oz) creamed coconut

500g (1lb 2oz) cooked lamb, cut into bite-sized pieces

115g (4 oz) frozen peas

salt and freshly ground black pepper

chopped coriander, to garnish

METHOD

1 Place the onions, garlic, ginger, green peppers, and chilli in a blender with 1 tablespoon of water and blend to a purée.

2 Heat 1 tablespoon of oil in a large saucepan or flameproof casserole, add the mustard seeds and fry, stirring, for 30 seconds, or until they begin to pop. Pour in the onion purée, increase the heat, and allow to bubble, stirring frequently, for 3–5 minutes, or until all the water has evaporated and the purée is thick and fairly dry.

3 Add the remaining oil and curry powder, and stir-fry for 30 seconds, then add the tomatoes with their juice, and 75ml (2½fl oz) water. Cook for 1 minute, stirring constantly, then add the coconut, and stir until well incorporated.

4 Add the lamb and peas and bring back to boiling point, then reduce the heat, cover, and simmer for 10–15 minutes, until heated through. Season to taste with salt and pepper, garnish with chopped coriander, and serve with rice or naan bread.

serves 4

prep 15 mins
• cook 25 mins

blender

freeze for
up to 3 months

Sausage and mustard casserole

This casserole is pure winter bliss. For an added twist, try it with a variety of sausages.

INGREDIENTS

1 tbsp olive oil

12 good-quality pork sausages

1 large onion, thinly sliced

225g (8 oz) small chestnut mushrooms

1 cooking apple, peeled, cored, and cut into chunks

1 bay leaf

1 tbsp chopped sage

300ml (10fl oz) chicken stock

2 tsp Dijon mustard

1 tsp wholegrain mustard

1 tsp made English mustard

150ml (5fl oz) double cream

salt and freshly ground black pepper

METHOD

1 Heat the oil in the casserole and gently fry the sausages until golden all over. Remove the sausages with a slotted spoon and set aside.

2 Add the onion to the casserole and cook until softened. Add the mushrooms and cook for 5 minutes, then stir in the apple, bay leaf, sage, and stock.

3 Bring to the boil, then return the sausages to the casserole. Reduce the heat, cover, and cook gently for 20 minutes, stirring often. The apple pieces should break down and thicken the sauce slightly. If they are still holding their shape, mash them with the back of a wooden spoon and stir in.

4 Mix the mustards and cream together in a bowl, and season with salt and pepper. Pour into the casserole, increase the heat, and boil gently for 5 minutes, or until the sauce has thickened slightly. Serve with creamy mashed potato and steamed cabbage.

serves 6

prep 15 mins
• cook 45 mins

large flameproof casserole

Spanish stew

Known as *Cocido* in Spain, this is a complete one-pot meal.

INGREDIENTS

4 tbsp olive oil

4 small onions, quartered

2 garlic cloves, sliced

4 thick slices belly pork, about 500g
(1lb 2oz) in total

4 chicken thighs, about 300g
(10 oz) in total

250g (9 oz) beef braising steak,
cut into 4 slices

175g (6 oz) tocino or smoked streaky
bacon, cut into 4 pieces

4 small pork spare ribs, 150g (5½ oz)
total weight

100ml (3½fl oz) white wine

175g (6 oz) chorizo, cut into 4 pieces

175g (6 oz) morcilla (Spanish black pudding)

small ham bone

1 bay leaf

salt and freshly ground black pepper

8 small waxy potatoes

4 carrots, halved lengthways

400g can chickpeas, drained

1 Savoy cabbage or green cabbage
heart, quartered

3 tbsp chopped flat-leaf parsley, to garnish

METHOD

1 Heat 1 tablespoon of oil in a large saucepan with the onions and garlic and fry for
10 minutes, stirring occasionally. Heat the remaining oil in a frying pan and fry the
pork, chicken, beef, tocino or bacon, and spare ribs in batches until lightly browned
on all sides, then transfer to the pan with the onions.

2 Add the wine into the frying pan, reduce by half, then pour into the saucepan. Add the
chorizo, morcilla, ham bone, and bay leaf to the saucpan, season to taste with salt and
pepper, then pour in enough cold water to cover. Bring to boil, then simmer, covered,
for 1 hour 30 minutes. Add the potatoes and carrots to the pan, continue to cook for
30 minutes, then add the chickpeas and cabbage, and cook for 15 minutes.

3 To serve, remove the bay leaf and ham bone and divide the meat and vegetables
between serving plates. Add a few spoonfuls of the hot broth to each and sprinkle
with parsley.

serves 6–8

prep 25 mins
• cook 2 hrs 45 mins

Burgundy beef

In this classic French casserole, *Boeuf Bourguignon*, long, slow braising ensures the meat becomes tender.

INGREDIENTS

175g (6 oz) streaky bacon rashers, chopped

1–2 tbsp oil

900g (2lb) braising steak, cut into 4cm (1½in) cubes

12 small shallots

1 tbsp plain flour

300ml (10fl oz) red wine

300ml (10fl oz) beef stock

115g (4 oz) button mushrooms

1 bay leaf

1 tsp dried herbes de Provence

salt and freshly ground black pepper

4 tbsp flat-leaf parsley, chopped

mashed potatoes, to serve

METHOD

1 Preheat the oven to 160°C (325°F/Gas 3). Fry the bacon in a non-stick frying pan until lightly browned. Drain on kitchen paper and transfer to a casserole.

2 Depending on how much fat is left from the bacon, add a little oil to the pan if necessary so that you have about 2–3 tablespoons. Fry the beef in batches over a high heat, transferring to the casserole as they brown.

3 Reduce the heat to medium and fry the shallots. Transfer to the casserole and stir the flour into the remaining fat in the frying pan. If the pan is quite dry, mix the flour with a little of the wine or stock. Pour the wine and stock into the frying pan and bring to the boil, stirring constantly until smooth.

4 Add the mushrooms, bay leaf, and dried herbs. Season to taste with salt and pepper and pour the contents of the pan over the meat and shallots in the casserole. Cover and cook in the oven for 2 hours, or until the meat is very tender.

5 Sprinkle with chopped parsley and serve hot with mashed potatoes.

 serves 4

 prep 25 mins • cook 2 hrs 30 mins

 freeze for up to 3 months

Spiced beans and herb hash

This medley of chopped potatoes and chilli beans makes a hearty breakfast or brunch.

INGREDIENTS

1 tsp olive oil
knob of butter
1 red onion, roughly chopped
salt and freshly ground black pepper
handful of thyme sprigs, leaves picked
450g (1lb) floury potatoes, peeled
  and cubed
400g can chilli mixed beans
150ml (5fl oz) hot vegetable stock
handful of flat-leaf parsley,
  finely chopped

METHOD

1 Heat the oil and butter in a non-stick frying pan over a low heat. Add the onion, a pinch of salt, and the thyme leaves, and sweat for about 5 minutes until the onion is soft.

2 Add the potatoes, and sauté until beginning to turn golden – you may need to add more olive oil.

3 When the potatoes are nearly cooked – after about 15 minutes – tip in the mixed beans, and stir together. Pour in the hot stock, and simmer for 10 minutes. Stir through the parsley, and season well with salt and pepper. Serve hot.

serves 4

prep 10 mins
• cook 30 mins

Beef and leek couscous

Filling enough to be served as a main course, this is a convenient dish for feeding a hungry crowd.

INGREDIENTS

8 tbsp olive oil

6 leeks, finely sliced

675g (1½lb) minced beef

2 red chillies, deseeded and
 finely chopped

2 tsp paprika

6 garlic cloves, sliced

150ml (5fl oz) dry white wine

450ml (15fl oz) hot beef stock

handful of flat-leaf parsley,
 finely chopped

450g (1lb) couscous

METHOD

1 Preheat the oven to 150°C (300°F/Gas 2). Heat the oil in a large heavy-based pan, add the leeks, and cook over a medium heat for 5 minutes. Add the mince and cook, stirring occasionally, for 10 minutes, or until no longer pink.

2 Stir in the chillies, paprika, and garlic and cook for 2 minutes. Pour in the wine and cook for 3 minutes, then add the stock and parsley and combine well. Stir in the couscous, then cover with a lid and cook in the oven for 15 minutes. Stir well and serve.

serves 6–8

prep 25 mins
• cook 30 mins

Sweet potato and butterbean stew

A satisfying vegetarian supper dish that is heavenly on winter evenings.

INGREDIENTS

450g (1lb) sweet potatoes,
  peeled and cut into thick slices
2 tbsp maple syrup
1 tbsp olive oil
1 red onion, finely chopped
1 tsp cumin seeds
salt and freshly ground black pepper

400g can peeled whole plum
  tomatoes, chopped
splash of balsamic vinegar
400g can butterbeans, drained and rinsed
handful of Swiss chard or spinach leaves
150ml (5fl oz) Greek-style yogurt
handful of mint leaves, to garnish

METHOD

1 Cook the sweet potatoes and maple syrup in a large wide pan of boiling salted water for 10 minutes until tender, but not too soft. Drain well, set aside, and keep warm.

2 Meanwhile, heat the oil in a large wide pan or deep frying pan over a low heat. Add the onion, cumin seeds, and a pinch of salt, and sweat for about 5 minutes until the onion is soft and translucent. Tip in the tomatoes, including any juices, and the balsamic vinegar, and cook for about 10 minutes. Taste, and season with salt and pepper.

3 Add the butterbeans, and simmer for a further 5 minutes, then stir through the Swiss chard or spinach. Cook for a couple of minutes more until the leaves just wilt. Remove from the heat, and top with the sweet potatoes. Preheat the grill to hot.

4 Transfer to an ovenproof dish, top with yogurt, and grill until golden. Garnish with mint leaves.

serves 4

prep 10 mins
• cook 30 mins

Daube of beef with wild mushrooms

This rich stew benefits from being made a few days before serving so the flavours can develop.

INGREDIENTS

2 tbsp olive oil

30g (1 oz) butter

900g (2lb) chuck steak, cut into 7.5cm (3in) pieces

2 tbsp plain flour

salt and freshly ground black pepper

115g (4 oz) rindless bacon rashers, chopped

2 small onions, finely chopped

3 garlic cloves, crushed

1 celery stick, finely chopped

3 carrots, diced

1 tbsp chopped fresh or dried thyme

900ml (1½ pints) red wine

2 tbsp brandy (optional)

zest and juice of 1 orange

175g (6 oz) field mushrooms

30g (1 oz) dried mushrooms

1 tbsp tomato purée

METHOD

1 Heat the olive oil and butter in the casserole. Coat the meat in seasoned flour, then brown on all sides in the casserole. Remove the pieces to a warm plate.

2 Fry the bacon, onions, garlic, and celery in the casserole, until lightly coloured. Stir in the beef along with the carrots and thyme. Pour in the red wine, the brandy, and the orange zest and juice; bring to the boil, stirring, then reduce the heat, cover, and simmer for 1 hour.

3 Meanwhile, clean and slice the field mushrooms. Put the dried mushrooms in a bowl and pour over boiling water. Leave to soak for 15 minutes, then drain, dry, and chop. Stir the mushrooms and the tomato purée into the casserole.

4 Cover and continue to simmer for another 30 minutes, or until the meat is very tender. Serve while still hot with boiled potatoes, fried bread triangles, and a sprinkling of chopped flat-leaf parsley.

serves 6

prep 30 mins • cook 2 hrs

flameproof casserole with a tight-fitting lid

freeze for up to 3 months

Autumn game casserole

Mixed game makes a wonderfully rich-flavoured dish. Look for ready-diced packs of meat, which cut down on preparation time.

INGREDIENTS

2 tbsp olive oil

500g (1lb 2oz) mixed casserole game, such as pheasant, partridge, venison, rabbit, and pigeon, diced

1 onion, sliced

1 carrot, sliced

1 parsnip, sliced

1 fennel bulb, sliced, leaves reserved

2 tbsp plain flour

200ml (7fl oz) dry cider or apple juice

200ml (7fl oz) chicken stock

250g (9 oz) chestnut mushrooms, thickly sliced

½ tsp fennel seeds

salt and freshly ground black pepper

METHOD

1 Preheat the oven to 160°C (325°C/Gas 3). Heat the oil in a flameproof casserole and fry the diced meats, stirring occasionally, for 3–4 minutes, or until lightly browned. Remove and keep hot.

2 Add the onion, carrot, parsnip, and sliced fennel to the casserole and fry, stirring occasionally, for 4–5 minutes, or until lightly coloured. Sprinkle in the flour and gradually stir in the cider and stock. Add the mushrooms and fennel seeds, then return the meat to the casserole.

3 Season well and bring to the boil. Cover tightly with a lid and place in the oven for 1 hour 20 minutes, or until the meat and vegetables are tender.

4 Sprinkle the casserole with the reserved fennel leaves, and serve hot.

 serves 4

 prep 20 mins • cook 1 hr 30 mins

 flameproof casserole

 freeze for up to 3 months

Rosemary and chilli sausages with new potatoes

This roast is flavourful and extremely easy to do – it's ideal for lazy Sundays.

INGREDIENTS

8–12 good-quality pork sausages
2 red onions, peeled and cut
  into eighths
pinch of chilli flakes
handful of rosemary stalks
1.1kg (2½lb) new potatoes,
  large ones halved
salt and freshly ground
  black pepper
1 tbsp olive oil

METHOD

1 Preheat the oven to 200°C (400°F/Gas 6). Put the sausages in a roasting tin along with the onion, sprinkle over the chilli flakes and rosemary, then add the new potatoes. Season well with salt and pepper, then drizzle over the oil and combine everything together well.

2 Put in the oven to roast for 30–40 minutes, or until the sausages are golden all over and cooked through. Turn the sausages and potatoes halfway through cooking.

serves 4

prep 15 mins
• cook 40 mins

Arroz con pollo

This is a colourful chicken and rice dish from Latin America.

INGREDIENTS

2 tbsp olive oil

8 chicken thighs

1 Spanish onion, finely sliced

1 green pepper, deseeded and chopped

1 red pepper, deseeded and chopped

2 garlic cloves, finely chopped

1 tsp smoked paprika

1 bay leaf

230g can chopped tomatoes

1 tsp thyme leaves

1 tsp dried oregano

175g (6 oz) long-grain rice

pinch of saffron threads

750ml (1¼ pints) chicken stock

2 tbsp tomato purée

juice of ½ lemon

salt and freshly ground black pepper

100g (3½ oz) frozen peas

METHOD

1 Preheat the oven to 180°C (350°F/Gas 4). Heat half the oil in a large flameproof casserole and fry the chicken thighs over high heat, turning frequently, or until evenly browned. Remove from the casserole, drain on kitchen paper, and set aside.

2 Add the remaining oil, reduce the heat, and fry the onion until softened. Add the chopped peppers and garlic and fry for 5 minutes, or until they start to soften. Add the paprika, bay leaf, chopped tomatoes, thyme, and oregano, and stir in the rice. Fry for 1–2 minutes, stirring constantly.

3 Crumble in the saffron, add the stock, tomato purée, and lemon juice, and season to taste with salt and pepper.

4 Return the chicken thighs to the casserole, pushing them down into the rice, cover, and cook in the oven for 15 minutes. Remove the casserole from the oven, add the peas and return to the oven for a further 10 minutes, or until the rice is tender and has absorbed the cooking liquid. Serve hot, straight from the casserole.

serves 4

prep 20 mins
• cook 45 mins

large flameproof casserole

Malaysian-style chicken with noodles

INGREDIENTS

8 large chicken pieces (breasts, legs, and thighs), about 1.1kg (2½lb) in weight, or 1 large chicken, jointed

salt and freshly ground black pepper

5 red chillies, deseeded

2 tbsp curry powder

2 tsp turmeric

2 tsp ground cumin

6 garlic cloves, grated or finely chopped

8 shallots, finely chopped

3 tbsp vegetable oil or sunflower oil

2 x 400g cans coconut milk

2 tsp sugar

6 tomatoes, skinned and chopped

1 red onion, finely chopped

handful of coriander leaves, chopped, plus extra to garnish

600ml (1 pint) chicken stock

450g (1lb) thick egg noodles

1 tbsp vegetable oil, for frying

METHOD

1 Season the chicken well with salt and pepper and put to one side. Put the chillies, curry powder, turmeric, cumin, garlic, shallots, and oil in a food processor, and whiz to a smooth paste.

2 Heat a large heavy-based pan, add the paste, and cook over a medium heat for 5 minutes, stirring frequently. Add the chicken pieces skin-side down and cook for 10 minutes, or until evenly browned. Turn halfway through cooking.

3 Shake the cans of coconut milk before opening, then add the milk to the pan along with the sugar. Season well with salt and pepper, bring to the boil, then reduce the heat and allow to simmer for 20 minutes, or until the coconut mixture has reduced down. Add the tomatoes and onion and cook for 10 minutes more, then stir in the coriander. Cover and leave to stand while you prepare the noodles.

4 Put the stock in a large pan of hot water and bring to the boil. Add the noodles and cook for 8 minutes, or until almost cooked but not too soft. Drain well. Heat the oil in a wok or deep frying pan, add the noodles, and cook for 3 minutes. Season well with salt and pepper, then toss together well and transfer to a large shallow platter. Spoon over the chicken and sauce, garnish with the remaining coriander, and serve.

serves 8

prep 15 mins
• cook 1 hr

food processor;
wok

Roast sweet potato and chilli tortilla

Spice up a Spanish tortilla with a couple of new ingredients.

INGREDIENTS

550g (1¼lb) sweet potatoes,
    peeled and cut into 2cm (¾in) cubes
1 tsp chilli flakes
5 tbsp olive oil
2 onions, finely chopped
6 eggs
salt and freshly ground black pepper

METHOD

1 Preheat the oven to 200°C (400°F/Gas 6). Put the sweet potatoes in a non-stick baking tray, add the chilli flakes and 2 tablespoons of the oil, and mix well. Roast for 30 minutes, or until browning, turning occasionally.

2 Meanwhile, put the remaining oil in a deep-sided frying pan, add the onions, and fry over a medium heat for 5 minutes, or until soft and translucent. Add the sweet potato, combine well, and leave to cool.

3 Break the eggs into a mixing bowl, season with salt and pepper, and beat well with a fork. Pour on to the potato and onion mixture, combine well, and cook over a low heat for 10 minutes, or until beginning to set. Transfer the pan to the oven, and cook for a further 10 minutes, or until the top is golden. Turn out on to a plate, and serve with a mixed salad.

serves 4–6

prep 15 mins,
• cook 45 mins

Pork with rice and tomatoes

Big, bold, and filling – this makes a super family meal.

INGREDIENTS

6 tbsp olive oil

3 onions, diced

1.1kg (2½lb) lean pork, cut into 5cm
  (2in) chunks

6 garlic cloves, grated or finely chopped

handful of flat-leaf parsley, chopped

1 tbsp thyme leaves

1 tbsp chopped sage leaves

2 tsp paprika

150ml (5fl oz) dry white wine

550g (1¼lb) long-grain rice

4 x 400g cans chopped tomatoes

salt and freshly ground black pepper

METHOD

1 Preheat the oven to 150°C (300°F/Gas 2). Heat the oil in a large heavy-based pan, add the onions, and cook over a medium heat for 5 minutes, or until starting to soften. Add the pork and cook, stirring occasionally, for 5 minutes, or until no longer pink. Add the garlic, parsley, thyme, sage, and paprika and combine well, then add the wine and cook for 5 minutes. Add the rice and tomatoes, stir to combine, then season well with salt and pepper.

2 Cover with a lid and cook in the oven for 1 hour. Stir occasionally and add a little hot water if it starts to dry out. Remove from the oven and allow to stand for 10 minutes with the lid on before serving.

serves 6–8

prep 30 mins
• cook 1 hr

Chicken stir-fried with spring onion, basil, and lemongrass

Cornflour gives the chicken a light, crispy coating to complement the fresh flavours of this healthy stir-fry.

INGREDIENTS

2–3 skinless chicken breast fillets,
  sliced into strips
salt and freshly ground black pepper
1 tbsp cornflour
2 tbsp sesame oil or vegetable oil
1 bunch of spring onions,
  sliced diagonally

3 garlic cloves, sliced
1 stalk lemongrass, tough outer
  leaves removed and chopped
2 red chillies, deseeded and sliced
1 tbsp Chinese rice wine
handful of basil leaves

METHOD

1 Season the chicken with salt and pepper. Put the cornflour on a plate, and toss the chicken strips in it until very well coated.

2 Heat 1 tablespoon of the oil in a wok over a high heat. Swirl the oil around the wok, then add the chicken and stir-fry quickly, moving the chicken around the wok for 3–5 minutes until golden and cooked through. Remove with a slotted spoon, and set aside. Keep warm.

3 Carefully wipe out the wok with kitchen paper, reduce the heat to medium-high, and add the remaining oil. When hot, add the spring onions, garlic, lemongrass, and chillies. Stir-fry for a couple of minutes, then increase the heat to high once again, and add the rice wine. Let it boil for a few minutes.

4 Return the chicken to the wok to just heat through, stir in the basil, and serve immediately with some fluffy rice.

serves 4

prep 10 mins
• cook 15 mins

wok

Gado gado

Literally meaning "mix mix", this is a traditional Indonesian dish of vegetables tossed with a tasty peanut sauce.

INGREDIENTS

4 corn on the cob

350g (12 oz) green beans, trimmed

550g (1¼lb) potatoes, unpeeled

450g (1lb) roasted peanuts

4 garlic cloves

3 red chillies, deseeded

salt and freshly ground black pepper

2 tsp demerara sugar

juice of 1 lime

4 carrots, finely sliced

200g (7 oz) beansprouts

half a cucumber, chopped into
  bite-sized pieces

6 eggs, hard-boiled, shelled,
  and quartered

handful of
  coriander, chopped

METHOD

1 Cook the corn on the cob in a pan of boiling salted water for 6–8 minutes, or until soft. Add the green beans for the last 5 minutes of cooking. Drain, slice the corn on the cob into chunky rings, and place in a large shallow serving bowl. Meanwhile, cook the potatoes in a pan of boiling salted water for 15 minutes, or until just beginning to soften. Drain and put to one side to cool, then slice and add to the sweetcorn and beans.

2 Put the peanuts, garlic, and chillies in a food processor and whiz until finely ground. Season with salt and pepper. Add a little water and whiz again to make a paste. Add the sugar and lime juice and whiz again, adding more water, if needed – the paste should be smooth but not too runny.

3 Add the carrots, beansprouts, and cucumber to the cooked vegetables, then pour over the sauce and toss together. Top with the hard-boiled eggs and coriander, and serve.

serves 8

prep 20 mins
• cook 20 mins

food processor

Bulgur wheat with prawns, okra, and dill

Okra is a tropical vegetable widely used in African, Caribbean, Indian, and Middle Eastern cuisines.

INGREDIENTS

400g (14 oz) bulgur wheat
8 tbsp olive oil
2 large onions, finely diced
400g (14 oz) okra, trimmed
6 garlic cloves, grated or finely chopped
675g (1½lb) (shelled weight) uncooked
  prawns, peeled and deveined
1 glass of dry white wine
large handful of dill, chopped
salt and freshly ground black pepper

METHOD

1 Preheat the oven to 150°C (300°F/Gas 2). Put the bulgur wheat in a bowl, and pour in enough boiling water to cover. Cover with a tea towel, leave for 5 minutes, then stir.

2 Meanwhile, heat the oil in a large heavy-based pan, add the onions, and cook over a medium heat for 5 minutes, or until starting to soften. Add the okra and cook for 2 minutes, then add the garlic and prawns and cook, stirring frequently, for 5 minutes, or until the prawns have turned pink.

3 Stir in the wine and dill and cook for 5 minutes, then stir in the bulgur wheat. Transfer to an ovenproof dish, cover with foil, and season with salt and pepper. Cook in the oven for 20 minutes, stirring occasionally. Serve with a mixed salad.

serves 8

prep 15 mins
• cook 40 mins

Spicy pork with chickpeas and tomatoes

Chickpeas lend a satisfying texture and an earthy flavour to this simple pork dish.

INGREDIENTS

8 tbsp olive oil

2 large onions, finely sliced

675g (1½lb) minced pork

6 garlic cloves, finely sliced

juice of 2 lemons

2 tsp cayenne pepper

2 x 400g cans chickpeas, drained
and rinsed

large handful of flat-leaf parsley,
finely chopped

6 large tomatoes, chopped

METHOD

1 Heat the oil in a large heavy-based pan, add the onions, and cook over a medium heat for 5 minutes, or until starting to soften. Add the mince and cook, stirring frequently, for 5 minutes, or until no longer pink.

2 Stir in the garlic, lemon juice, and cayenne, and cook for 1 minute. Add the chickpeas and parsley, stir well, then cook for 5 minutes. Add the tomatoes, combine well, then simmer for 15 minutes, stirring occasionally. Serve with a crisp green salad and fresh crusty bread.

serves 6–8

**prep 15 mins
• cook 30 mins**

INDEX

London, New York, Melbourne, Munich, and Delhi

Senior Editor Ros Walford

Editorial Assistant Shashwati Tia Sarkar

Designer Elma Aquino

Jacket Designer Mark Penfound

Senior DTP Designer David McDonald

Production Editor Kavita Varma

Indexer Dorothy Frame

DK INDIA

Editorial Consultant Dipali Singh

Designer Neha Ahuja

DTP Designer Tarun Sharma

DTP Coordinator Sunil Sharma

Head of Publishing Aparna Sharma

First published in Great Britain in 2012.
Material in this publication was previously published
in *The Cooking Book, 2008* and *Cook Express, 2009*
by Dorling Kindersley Limited
80 Strand, London WC2R oRL

Penguin (UK)

Copyright © 2008, 2009, 2012 Dorling Kindersley
Text copyright © 2008, 2009, 2012 Dorling Kindersley

10 9 8 7 6 5 4 3 2
002-177136-May/12

A CIP catalogue record for this book is available from the
British Library.

ISBN 978-1-4093-7495-4

Printed and bound by Hung Hing, China.